Who Do Yo

Think You Ar

The Power of BELIEVING in Yoursel

Nicholas Dillon, MS, MAED

The BELIEVE Coach | Educator | Consultant | Speaker

Copyright © 2012 by Nicholas Dillon

ISBN 978-0-7414-8004-0 Paperback
ISBN 978-0-7414-8005-7 Audiobook
ISBN 978-0-7414-8006-4 eBook

Printed in the United States of America

Published December 2012

INFINITY PUBLISHING
1094 New DeHaven Street, Suite 100
West Conshohocken, PA 19428-2713
Toll-free (877) BUY BOOK
Local Phone (610) 941-9999
Fax (610) 941-9959
Info@buybooksontheweb.com

To all those individuals who are survivors and overcomers of what life has dealt them up until this present moment. I challenge you to take a few moments to dust yourself off and tell yourself today that …

God is the source of my strength

Love is my religion; God is my example

Prosperity is my goal

Giving is always my purpose

Truth is my foundation

Success is just the next step

Healing happens every day

Favor follows me everywhere I go

Honesty is the key to my heart

Faith holds it all together

I AM what the Word says I am

I have what IT says I have

I believe all things are possible through Christ who strengthens me!

Acknowledgments

I would like to say a special thanks to the entire Dillon family and my close friends and associates for their love and support throughout this project. My life experiences have been a great inspiration for completing this project. I have received great support and lots of encouragement through my family, Life Coaching clients, professional network, and responses to my blog posts. Special thanks go out to my editors, attorneys, branding/marketing experts, and publishers for their hard work and efforts in getting this project ready for the public. Finally, thanks to Troy Rackley, a colleague, mentor, and friend, for his contribution to the project.

Contents

Foreword

I met Nick Dillon while networking on Facebook. When he told me that he had a passion for coaching, I really got inspired. As a professional coach myself, I find it amazing the discussions that you can get into with like-minded people. So, when Nick asked me to write the forward for his book, I felt honored. Nick has a passion for helping others achieve, and that is one of his drivers: helping others be successful. He is simply teaching us the way he learned himself.

When I read *Who Do You Think You Are?*, the thing that jumps out at me is how Nick wrote in such simple and easy-to-understand terms that you don't have to be a coach to understand it. He chose to write for laypeople, not just fellow coaches or HR practitioners.

Who Do You Think You Are? is a playbook that teaches you how to take charge of your life and also keep perspective as you shape your frame of reference to be what you want it to be for yourself—and not just for others.

As a coach, I learned a lot also because the exercises included in this book really bring it home and make you think. My favorite part was the BELIEVE model. This concept really allows you to understand that everything you believe is within your grasp. There is no magic bullet, but this guide helps us bring out the magic within us.

Who Do You Think You Are? asks all the right questions, but in order to make the change you want to make in your life, you must be ready to hear your answers to those questions. This simple guide will help you understand your frame of reference and start achieving what you set out to achieve.

This confirms to me that everyone should have a coach for themselves, and it starts with understanding the BELIEVE model and being open to your answers to the key questions.

Take it to the Next Level!

Troy Rackley

The Limitless You Expert—Speaker, Coach, Author

Preface

Who Do You Think You Are?

I start this book by asking that very personal question in order to get your attention and I don't happen to be sitting across from you in the comfort of your local coffeehouse.

I might put it another way. Do you ever wonder how well you know yourself? Are you ever uncomfortable with who you are—the individual you have become? Are there times when you question your feelings, emotions, or thoughts and where they might have come from? Do you ever find yourself questioning your relationships or your career choice? Are you sometimes baffled by your own behavior? If you answered yes to even one of these questions, then you're reading the right book.

The key to knowing who you are lies in a true understanding of what I call your *frame of reference*.

Your *frame of reference* is the sum total of the principles, values, and points of view you have picked up over a lifetime that now affect how you communicate and behave. More to the point, your frame of reference is where you are in your subconscious mind. It culminates to where you are in life, based on everything that has happened to you, and all the environmental and cultural influences that have made you the person that you are.

It's not a one size fit all concept. Each person will have their own unique set of circumstances that make up their frame of reference. It drives your thinking and behavior, and will impact everything we talk about throughout this book.

Here's some good news; your frame of reference is an ever-moving target that changes day to day. You can use it to mold and shape the person you want to be.

Whether you're confident or angry, sad or energetic, indifferent or ambitious—whatever the emotion—it's all tied to your frame of reference. The moment you identify who you are, you will be able to answer even the hardest questions: Why am I depressed? Why am I so driven? Why do I feel hopeless? Why are my relationships so stuck?

When I was a teenager, I didn't like who I was. I didn't feel loved. I was often bullied, lacked confidence, and had a very poor self-image. Why? My frame of reference had been shaped by the key concepts that I will speak on as you continue to read. As I begin to understand this "frame of reference" concept, I gained control over my view of myself and made the choice to see things through a newly defined perspective. Consider this; a boy who is brought up to accept the status quo is very likely to end up in a job he doesn't like as a man. A girl who is neglected by her parents might very well end up in an abusive relationship as a woman.

The point is this; there comes a time in our lives when we find ourselves reflecting on exactly how we got to where we are. The answer is straight forward—choices. The choices you've made throughout your life have gotten you to this place and time, just as surely as my choices have done the same.

If you're in a jail cell, you may be able to trace it back to the choices you made. If you're staring at a stack of bills and facing bankruptcy, it could be a reflection of past choices. If you've just been elected valedictorian of your graduating class, rest assured your choices impacted that outcome. If you've just been promoted, the same is true.

Everything you do in life is a choice. Every choice has ramifications and impacts your frame of reference at any given time.

Thinking—or not thinking—is directly related to the process of making choices. I have always taught my children to think through every decision to its logical conclusion before moving forward. Another father might encourage his child to rely on instinct. In both cases, those lessons will help shape the child's frames of reference and the choices they will make throughout their life.

If your parents assigned you weekly chores—mowing the lawn, taking out the trash, loading the dishwasher—you learned the value of responsibility. This value impacts your life. Identifying your frame of reference is a starting point in making choices and accepting *you* for who *you* are.

It is not enough to want your family and friends to love and accept you for whom you are; if you don't know who you are. You need to understand yourself and your life motivation. It is my goal to provide you with some concepts and life skills that will not only help you believe in yourself but also understand your frame of reference. Once found, you will be able to look yourself in the mirror and shout boldly to the world, "This is who I am!"

**B**elieve

Each day when you wake up, ask yourself, "What is my purpose?"

Your frame of reference will naturally dictate your purpose. Add the two together and you have your personal mission statement, that internal driver that provides you with a source of inspiration and feeling of significance. If the inspiration is positive, you're on a good track. If it's negative, you have to stop, evaluate your frame of reference, and make the decision to change.

An entrepreneur's success is based upon effort and a strong work ethic. If your frame of reference has been shaped by a steady diet of entitlement, you will struggle and be constantly challenged until you choose a different set of values.

One of my motivations for seeking a master's degree some years back was the desire to instill in my children the value of education. I wanted that belief in knowledge and personal development to be a part of how they would ultimately view themselves and their own life initiatives.

Throughout this book, I break down frame of reference and our search for who we are into several different concepts. If you look at each one, you will see that they are all derived from the word *believe*. I did this so that you start and end this book by *believing* in yourself and your ability to live your life to your greatest potential. Here is the breakdown of the BELIEVE Model:

B – The driving motivational force behind your BEHAVIOR

E – Your EMOTIONS and feelings

L – Your LIFE experiences

I – Your IMAGE of self

E – Your EXTENDED family and friends' support

V – Your VALUES and beliefs

E – Your ENVIRONMENT

As you consider the items listed above, you may seemingly find yourself reflecting on exactly what your frame of reference really is. At the end of each chapter you will find several assessment tools to help you reinforce behavioral change.

We start first by talking about behavior because each of the other letters in our BELIEVE paradigm directly impact and affect behavior. The emotions you feel, the impact of your life experiences, the image you've developed for yourself, the influences of your extended family, the things that you have grown to value, and the environment you were raised in or live in currently are all prominent in shaping your frame of reference each day of your life .

Why do we behave the way we do? Why do we think the way we think? Those are the questions we seek to answer in this book. Please keep them in mind. Once you have a grasp the BELIEVE concepts, you will no longer have to question why you do what you do. You will know. You will know why you shouted at your spouse or threw a fit at work. You will know why people are drawn to your leadership skills or seek your advice on difficult questions.

My professional career has placed me in several of harshest correctional institutions in the country. I have also had the opportunity to work with individuals who may be out on probation or parole. I found that most of the men with this history of background consider themselves products of their environments. They will tell you that they are who they are because of circumstances beyond their control. They are perpetually angry. This is their frame of reference and they don't see any way out. They don't believe they have choices. They don't believe they can alter their frame of reference or control their behavior. Then we sit down and begin talking; in time, it becomes clear that they *are* in control, that they *can* change their thinking, and they in fact hold the key to how they act and how they behave. It all requires a choice.

For these men, the system is not the answer; the system cannot change their behavior. Only they can. Society as a whole is not the answer either. The only solution is being able to understand yourself and your frame of reference. That understanding will provide you with some wisdom that you can use to dictate your future as you no longer need to define your future based on bad choices or external circumstances.

Once you grasp that, the next step is to own it. You have to decide what you intend to do with this new understanding. You have to be open for change, open for help, open to a new way of thinking. You have to be open to the idea of better choices and to the fact that the only person responsible for your behavior is you.

Emotions and Feelings

How are you feeling?

This is the first question you should ask yourself as you start the self-check on your frame of reference. Emotions and the meanings we attach to them can very often be the most honest of all life barometers in assessing how you are feeling.

Our emotions represent the reaction we have to some event, situation, or person. Our feelings represent our attitude at any given time.

All feelings have an emotional foundation. Therefore, how you *feel* is a result of the emotion you're experiencing.

If I say to you, "How are you doing?" and you say, "I'm great," there is a positive emotion tied to that feeling, a positive energy. If you're feeling sad or angry, the emotional reaction to those feelings will also manifest in your behavior. It will show on your face, in your posture, and in the tone of your voice.

So the question "How are you feeling?" is directly related to your frame of reference. It is easy enough to answer, "I'm fine," and leave it at that. But truly identifying the emotion driving your behavior takes a bit more effort. It requires some internal assessment. Ask yourself, "How am I *really* feeling," and then be totally honest with yourself.

In great measure, our quest to understand who we are is about believing in ourselves and being in touch with our feelings and emotions. They are the building blocks that can make us strong and positively impact our lives; so ignoring them in not an option.

Everything you do in life you do with one primary goal in mind: personal satisfaction. We don't intentionally do things that make us feel bad. Even if you're in a job that you dislike and you're staying in that job for financial gain, you are reaping something positive from it.

You wake up each day in the throes of a certain mood; no one wakes up with a blank slate. These feelings might be carried over from the previous day, or they might be the product of the sleep you got the night before. No matter where the mood came from, you want to feel good and avoid feeling bad. I say this so that you really grasp the fact that you have a choice about how you feel. You can mentally assign a feeling to each moment in each day, and you can decide how long or how short you want that feeling to last. This is a personal power too many of us fail to recognize. You honestly do not have to give into negativity if that is not the feeling or emotion you want to present.

It's not acceptable to say, "I'm depressed and don't know why." or "I'm angry and can't do anything about it." Yes, you can. There is an emotion that governs each of those feelings—a reaction to some event, situation, or person—and identifying your frame of reference requires you to seek out that emotion.

Let me reiterate again that we are each in charge of our feelings. We are in charge of our reactions to situations, circumstances, and other people. We can assign a feeling to any given moment. The more in tune you are with your frame of reference, the more influence you have over your feelings and emotions. Understanding this concept will give you increasing influence over your behavior.

We are all masters at masking our emotions. When was the last time you went to a party after having a fight with your spouse and acted as if nothing was bothering you? We have all gone to work after a restless night's sleep and put on the mask of the energetic and enterprising coworker.

Yes, there is a time and place for this kind of behavior, but the mask has to come off at some point. You have to go into your heart and be true to the emotions you feel. Otherwise, your search for who you really are will be derailed, and you'll constantly be starting over.

Make no mistake: emotions are tricky. The less in tune you are with them, the more they can rule your behavior through passing feelings.

I was counseling a couple recently, when it came to light that the man, whom we will refer to at Jim, soon after waking up in the morning, would often announce to his wife and anyone else who was listening , "Today's going to be a bad day." When I asked him why, his reply was, "I don't know. It's just one of those days."

We came to discover through ongoing conversation that he had simply made a decision. He had assigned a negative emotion, "I'm going to be miserable today." As we talked, he began to realize that the power of choice was *his*. He would ascribe an emotion, just as he had been doing, but the emotion could just as easily be a positive one instead of a negative one. His frame of reference—built upon thirty years of events and circumstances—had convinced him that bad days just happened and there was nothing he could do about it. Now, he realizes there is something he *could* do about it. He can choose.

This ability to choose was never more evident than with the many abuse victims I have counseled over the years. These men and women are some of the most powerful examples of how events and circumstances can hold you mentally captive and how emotions can trump all else. Victims of abuse often act from a point of reference that, if left unchecked, can leave them scarred for life. But those who have suffered abuse in the past do have a choice going forward. Instead of looking at themselves as victims, I encourage them to look at themselves as survivors. I say to them, "You are a new person because you're thinking differently. You're a survivor, strong and proud. In fact, here is an opportunity for you to become an ambassador for the movement against abuse and completely turn the tables on your past."

Imagine the effect such thinking can have on a person's behavior.

Never forget how closely connected your feelings are to your emotions, and never forget that they are sometimes at war with one another. For example, you're in a failing relationship, but the emotional fear of being alone won't allow you to think about moving on.

So what does this mean? It means that you need to think about who is winning the battle—which emotions are dominating your feelings and ultimately dictating your behavior? This has to be part of your daily self-check.

Saying, "My emotions got the best of me" is not a viable excuse for bad behavior. You do have control. You do have the strength of will to manage your feelings and to determine the direction your life will take. It begins with the inner dialogue or self-talk that happens on a daily basis.

Everything you think and do is meant to create circumstances in your life that allow you to feel good. On an even deeper level, the way you feel is determined largely by what you believe. That belief helps to shape your frame of reference for today—and for the future.

I encourage you to check in with your feelings and emotions each day without fail. If they are not positive, change them. Remember that you are the one choosing the feelings and assigning meaning to your emotions based on the experiences and circumstances. Use your energy and stay positive!

Self-Assessment: How Are You Feeling?

Over the next seven days, I would like you to make a note of how you are feeling at the start of each day. Pay special attention to what is actually fostering the feelings and make a note of that as well.

Example 1: I am feeling agitated. This agitation is the result of the negative job review I received at work yesterday.

Example 2: I am feeling excited. This excitement is fostered by the prospect of starting a new job today.

Day 1 _____

Day 2 _____

Day 3 _____

Day 4 _____

Day 5 _____

Day 6 _____

Day 7 _____

Each evening, spend a few minutes reflecting on your day. Did your feelings from the morning change, or did they remain consistent throughout the day. Why?

Example 1: I am still agitated. I had a very unproductive day, and it seemed like I was powerless to staying on task.

Example 2: I am even more excited and a bit overwhelmed. My new job is filled with new and challenging responsibilities, and my new coworkers seemed very positive.

Day 1 _____

Day 2 _____

Day 3 _____

Day 4 _____

Day 5 _____

Day 6 _____

Day 7 _____

Were the plans, goals, or tasks you had for the day affected by how you are or were feeling?

Example 1: I had every intention of being more productive, but I couldn't seem to overcome the anger from my poor review.

Example 2: Approaching the new job with an open mind allowed me to interact with my new team members in a positive, fun way.

Day 1 _____

Day 2 _____

Day 3 _____

Day 4 _____

Day 5 _____

Day 6 _____

Day 7 _____

Describe what motivating factors drove your feelings each day. If those factors were negative, try to think positively. Remember that you are in control of your thoughts and can assign any feeling or emotion you want to those thoughts and behave accordingly.

Example 1: I am going to think about what I can do to change my approach to my job and be more positive about my role at work.

Example 2: I want this new job to be a homerun. I intend to come to work every day determined to be the best team member I can be.

Day 1 _____

Day 2 _____

Day 3 _____

Day 4 _____

Day 5 _____

Day 6 _____

Day 7 _____

Feeling great brings about a positive emotion and allows you to attract positive energy in return. Set a goal of never allowing the negative attitudes or thoughts of others to bring you down. Focus on staying upbeat; then observe how good that healthy energy makes you feel.

With that in mind, make a list of any obstacles or circumstances in your life that you anticipate will affect your feelings over the next seven days. After you write out the list, develop an action plan with a goal of maximizing the positive energy you're feeling.

Example 1 Obstacle: My immediate boss (the one who wrote the negative job review) and I will be attending a three-day conference together this week.

Example 1 Action Plan: I will approach my boss beforehand and let him know how much I appreciate his feedback on my review, and I will use the three-day trip to shine.

Day 1 _____

Day 2 _____

Day 3 _____

Day 4 _____

Day 5 _____

Day 6 _____

Day 7 _____

Life Experiences

The next concept in our model comes from the letter "L" in the word BELIEVE: life experiences. Our experiences in life have ongoing importance in our search for who we really are.

It is impossible to deny the feelings and emotions that well up in my heart as I reflect back on my life. When I think about those bullying experiences of my teenage years, my mind re-processes that feeling of anxiety and loneliness. Graduating from high school saw a memorable moment of confidence and a desire to be able to free myself and accomplish something better for myself in life. I can feel the excitement of the experiences of my twenties and the later development of self-esteem and confidence. As I approached my thirties, I felt even more acceptance and warmth.

It is important to know that our life experiences, eventful or not, have a profound impact on our lives and play a huge role in the development of our frame of reference. Some experiences are so powerful that they can actually save your life. I was nearly driven to suicide by the loneliness and disconnect I felt as a teenager. It was several experiences that drove me to such a low point. However, I can also point directly to the religious teachings of my youth that had a positive long-term effect on my life and stayed my hand until those suicidal thoughts passed.

Your life experiences can create a frame of reference based upon despair and disillusionment or one founded upon inspiration and motivation. Your experiences can sustain you, or they can steal away your joy. The choice is yours. You just need to have the mental capacity to be able to manage those emotions and feeling.

One of the primary skills that I use with my clients is the power of life experiences and how they can and should be used to a person's advantage. For example, an apathetic, insensitive teacher can be as influential as an energetic, insightful one because you can use both experiences to affect change in your life. You can say, "I will never treat a young mind with the disinterest and disrespect that teacher did me."

Our life experiences not only shape our beliefs and our values, but they clearly impact the way we see ourselves. A child who takes the teasing of her peers so personally that she begins to see herself as unimportant and worthless has a deep hurt to ascend from later in life, but an acceptance and understanding of those experiences can provide the energy that makes the ascent possible.

This willingness to openly explore your life experiences is, in short, where the rubber meets the road when it comes to your quest to know who you are and to discover a deep belief in yourself. This is where you say to yourself, "I'm willing to revisit my past experiences and appreciate how and why they are affecting my behavior today."

Here is where you ask, "What emotions have I attached to these experiences? How can I use this newfound understanding to change my negative behavior or reinforce my positive behavior?"

You have the power of choice. You have the power to assign whatever meaning you choose to those experiences. For example, I can carry anger for many years after a traumatic experience or I can decide that I will no longer assign the emotion of anger but rather simply peace and solace.

Experiences surrounding family, employment, relationships, and even school will influence your thought processes every day and will likewise affect what you hold to be true about yourself.

Consider your life experiences, as an ongoing learning process. These experiences can be used as stepping-stones to where you see yourself going in life. They can just as readily be used to avoid roads you don't care to travel down again.

Whether we like it or not, we tend to mimic behavior we experienced in the past—from a parent, a sibling, a peer, or anyone else of influence in our lives. If you observed the horrors of spousal abuse, for example, you are far more likely to be an abuser yourself unless you consciously choose a different path. On the other hand, if your parents showed kindness to people of all stations in life, you are far more likely to do so yourself. Awareness in either case is the key. Affecting your behavior, in particular avoiding negative behavior, requires a deep-seated understanding and acceptance of your life experiences. You can't make the most of your frame of reference without this understanding and acceptance.

How do we do this? By fully appreciating that past experiences do *not* have to define our behavior today, tomorrow, or anytime, no matter how negative the experience. Everything is a choice.

Take for example the woman who grows up under the iron fist of an alcoholic father and who very consciously chooses neither to drink nor to associate with men who drink or have a history of being an abuser.

Take for example the man who is improperly branded as dumb or a slow learner as a child and later uses this inaccurate application of labels as incentive to start a foundation for gifted and talented children.

You are in a position to give each experience in your life meaning and decide what category you will assign to the experience: good, bad, or inconsequential; meaningful, purposeful, or insignificant. In any case, you will naturally archive these experiences and then utilize them to define your current frame of reference.

Some people are still healing from childhood experiences. Some are still waiting for their breakthrough moment, and, in the meantime, they hold onto those bad experiences and find it difficult to experience the many positive things that life has to offer.

I challenge you to take from your experiences only those positive things that will help you grow into the person you want to be. Lose or redefine those experiences that could potentially hold you back from achieving your greatness. It may not be easy, but it can be done one day at a time. Ultimately, a positive, clearly defined frame of reference is the key to living a purpose-driven life.

Self-Assessment: Describe Your Life Experiences

As you reflect on your life, describe some events that have had an impact on your life. Specifically, how have those experiences shaped your character, motivation, relationships, and the choices you make?

Example 1: I am confident, energetic, and free-spirited. I was fortunate to watch my father run a successful business, and I came away from the experience with a strong work ethic and a desire to contribute positively to my community.

_____

_____

_____

_____

_____

Write down at least one extremely positive experience you have had in life that you will cherish forever (i.e. a special celebration, a memorable holiday, a work promotion, or a great relationship). After doing so, just think about how that experience made you feel and how it continues to make you feel. Bottle up the feeling and emotion you gave that experience, and open that bottle when you have an experience that makes you feel differently.

Example 2: I will always cherish the birth of our first child. There was a consuming sense of pride and awe in bringing new life into the world, and there was overpowering discovery of love far deeper than anything I ever expected to feel.

_____

_____

_____

_____

_____

Write down at least one extremely negative life experience (i.e., a failed relationship, an episode of physical or mental abuse, a school incident, an accident, etc.) you may have had in life that you would just as soon forget. Think about how that experience made you feel, or even continues to make you feel. Now I want you to think for a moment. Know that you are a survivor of that experience. Take from that experience any positive light you can, knowing that even a pinhole of light in a dark room is a lodestar worth focusing on. Assign new meaning to that experience and write down how you want to remember it going forward.

Example 3: I was bullied in school and never once fought back against my aggressors. I became a target. I withdrew, and my last year in grade school was the worst of my life. It was only later, when I realized how insecure the boys who bullied me were, that I began to understand why it happened. It wasn't me; it was them. Now, as a teacher, I use the experience to spot potential bullying situations and use them as teaching moments.

_____

_____

_____

_____

_____

Image of Self

Understanding our frame of reference and being able to take charge of our behavior is tied directly to our image of self, the "I" in our BELIEVE model. Our self-image is something we are cognizant of the moment we wake up in the morning and see ourselves in the mirror. The reflections you see staring back at you is actually who you believe you are.

We can never really know who we are without an accurate understanding of the vision we have created of our self-image. Not surprisingly, this vision of influence impacts our frame of reference, which shows you how closely the two are intertwined. Both frame of reference and self-image are derived from our past experiences, from the environment in which we were raised, from the various support systems that have influenced our lives, and from the values and beliefs that we have developed over time.

These influences become what we hold to be our reality and very often determine our personal potential. The truth is you can achieve only what you believe you can achieve; if you choose to be held on to a traumatic experience of your past, your self-image will reflect that, and so will your behavior.

While most of us agree that it is important to have acquired a good self-image, too often we haven't. Some of us even wonder how we came into our self-image in the first place. It's a good question.

Your self-image starts to form during your early childhood. As you grow and develop (considering your environment, support, and experiences), you start to store messages (positive and negative) that you receive about yourself. Over the years, these messages are collected in your impressionable subconscious mind and create what will become your self-image. Think of how we were influenced by the nurturing—or lack thereof—that we received when we were young. Think of the impressions made upon us by our parents and siblings, our teachers and spiritual mentors, friends, and peers.

The father of a woman I have come to admire had a unique way of addressing her as a child. He would say, "You're big and ugly enough. You can do it." Imagine hearing that every day of your life. Instead of crawling into a hole, this woman used the phrase to motivate herself. She built a remarkably successful business when everyone told her she couldn't and wrote an autobiography titled—you guessed it—*Big and Ugly Enough.*

The bottom line is this: whether you were nurtured or not, you have a question to answer as you move through your life. Do you want to be what someone else says you are, or do you want to live a life of the greatness you aspire to have?

I recently counseled a boy who grew up with a speech condition that limited his ability to express himself verbally. This disability led to considerable alienation from his peers and schoolmates. When I met him, his self-image was not complimentary. Once we discovered the source of his poor self-esteem and lack of confidence, I didn't coddle him. I challenged him, saying, "Now it's time to look in the mirror and decide whether your past is going to rule your life or whether you're going to use this new awareness to become the person you want to be."

He took the challenge. He faced his demons and chose not to be held under mental bondage by them. Today he is a successful teacher and even more successful family man.

What I find to be so interesting is that even when we know our self-image is not what we want it to be; we are very reluctant to change the beliefs behind it. It is as though our self-image is not open to questioning or reason. We just automatically believe our perceptions to be true. Why? Is it fear? Is it doubt? Is it a lack of self-confidence?

If you believe you lack self-confidence and will never be successful; if you don't believe you have the ability to create really good relationships—whatever the belief—you will defend it to the end, even to yourself. Those messages you were programmed with as a child, or even as an adult, become so powerful that they define your self-image to the point that you are afraid to confront it or change it.

But make no mistake: you are in control. You cannot throw up your hands and say, "It is what it is." No. "It is what you decide to make it." You can make change happen. The amount of influence you allow your environment or your experiences to have over you is completely up to you. It is simply an excuse to claim that you've been dealt a bad hand and all you can do is play it out. Once again, I say, "No." You can change the cards you hold, and you can decide how to play those cards.

I am throwing down the gauntlet. If you are not who you want to be, or are not living the life you want to live, start with a makeover of your self-image. Take action. Start with positive self-talk. Tell yourself:

I am smart

I am beautiful

I communicate well

I am a good leader

I bring positive energy to my relationships

The idea is to send your sub-conscious mind new messages to counter-act those old messages you no longer want to define who you are. Your self-image does not have to mirror who you really are today. You are not that collection of painful or limiting memories. Create new experiences. Be conscious of breaking old habits. Be particular about the environment you are in. Make sure the support system you have stays positive, both now and going forward. Create yourself a new self-image.

Remember that the greatest personal power you have is the power to choose your own thoughts, and it is those thoughts that will propel you toward the discovery of your greatness.

Self-Assessment: Self-Image

This is an exercise that I want you to do while standing in front of the mirror. I want you to stand there for at least three minutes while asking yourself this question: "How do I feel about me?" Write your answer here and then read it back to yourself in the mirror. Do you believe what you wrote? If so, great! If not, write it again. The point is to be completely and totally real with yourself. Once you've done that, real change is the next step.

Example 1: I see an unattractive woman. I see a woman with no confidence. I see a woman fearful of changing her living situation.

Example 2: I see a lovable, caring woman. I see an independent, spirited woman. Yes, I am uncertain about the future, but I am willing to face the unknown with gusto.

_____

_____

_____

_____

_____

Please finish this sentence. "For me, self-image is…" (Consider this to be part of your personal mission statement.)

Example 1: For me, self-image is having the confidence to be the best I can be.

Example 2: For me, self-image is the ability to know and love myself.

_____

_____

_____

_____

_____

How much is your self-image influenced by how others see you? While we appreciate the input of others—including our support system—we want to make sure that the influence we get from these folks is positive and really works to complement our self-image positively. List the most important and positive support system you have. Then think about how you can enhance or expand this group.

Example 1: The AA is probably my most important support group. With that in mind, I should try and bring this same camaraderie to my inner circle.

Example 2: My most positive support comes from my immediate family. With that in mind, I should try and reach out to my friends more often as well.

_____

_____

_____

_____

_____

Top 10 Tips for Improving Your Self-Image

- Start speaking more positively to yourself. Use positive self-talk to get rid of any negative programs you have stored in your subconscious for years.

- Make a list of things you like about yourself, including those that others may have acknowledged about you.

- Since God made us all, accept who you are outwardly and continue to work on yourself on the inside.

- Realign yourself with a support system of family and friends that supports and values you. Do not compromise your personal values and beliefs.

- Trust yourself enough to accept the compliments of others.

- Smile! It looks good on you!

- Consider your body, mind, and spirit, and work on these three daily so that they remain healthy.

- Love yourself and embrace your differences.

- Maintain positive body language and be mindful of your nonverbal communication.

- Do not dwell on your past experiences. Think positive and become a lifelong learner. Forward thinking is a lot less stressful.

Extended Family and Support

Who do you think you are? That is the question we posed on the very first page of this book, and it is essential to understand just how much the support of extended family plays into the exploration of this question. Examining the support of family and friends is also critical to identifying our frame of reference and understanding why we think and behave a certain way. Extended family goes beyond our mom, dad, sister and brother, but rather includes other supportive influences such as guardians and caregivers.

Search your memory as far back as you can and gauge the quality of support you've had. Remember that our BELIEVE model up to this point is made up by our emotions and feelings, life experiences, and our image of ourselves. Now you will learn that you cannot fully believe in yourself without the support of our family. The question to consider is "Does my family believe in me as much as I believe in myself?"

Ideally, your immediate family—and yes, your extended family—should bring you the love and support you need throughout your life. This may not always the case. Family can sometimes have a negative influence on your life, and that is not the influence you want to drive your days, weeks, months, and years.

When the family bonds are positive, they link to our beginning and become a guide to our future. Unfortunately, the same can be said of negative family bonds. These early influences are fundamental to our individual development. In short, our parents and siblings have a lot to do with who we are today.

My childhood was a roller coaster of well-intended support and seeming emotional neglect. While I never questioned the commitment of my parents when it came to support, the level of influence my parents had on me was beyond respect but also included fear. This fear that was created in my subconscious had no voice and therefore did not foster the best relationship I believe I could have had. One of the impacting influences my mom maintains to this day was her commitment to education. Her philosophy was heard loud and clear, "You're smart. You can do it. You will do it. You can expect to excel in it."

She encouraged, she cajoled, and she helped when help was necessary. Even when I was away at college, I knew I could call her when classes got a little hard and she would be there—ready to crack the whip with one hand or deliver an encouraging word with the other.

Everyone wants to belong and feel accepted. A sense of belonging is derived from the strong family bond; belonging is inherent in our makeup. When we do not get that feeling of belonging from our support system, we spend a lifetime chasing it through other things of the world. Family is where our roots take hold and from there we grow. We are molded within a unit, which prepares us for what we will experience out in the world and how we will react to those experiences. We also learn values at an early age and carry them with us throughout our life. But remember this: values can also be either good or bad.

When you have an environment and support system that is positive and nurturing, it prepares you to be a positive member of society and allows you to contribute in a meaningful way.

If, however, any part of that environment and support system is dysfunctional or stagnant, you may find yourself thrust into a mode of pure survival, in particular as a teenager or young adult. The questions you have to consider can be almost primitive in nature. How do I get by? How do I stay afloat? Who am I?

If a child ends up on the streets, he may come to acquire his value from this experience. If this child falls in with a gang who provides even the most distorted type of camaraderie, it translates into support. Why? We all need support in some fashion or another. How far can this go? If the gang sells drugs, a young teen may see the act not as a crime; but as a means of survival.

In fact, we become what we are taught, and breaking away from such a cycle is not easy. As a counselor, I have to meet all my clients mentally where they are in their lives, not where I think they should be.

I have to tap into their frame of reference as it currently is, respect that frame of reference, and then show them why their behavior is maladaptive—why what they're doing does not work in society. Then the task is to help them shift their values.

And yes, values can be shifted. If your environment and support system steered you toward a negative value system, the damage can be undone. However, merely saying, "You know that's wrong" does not work given the socialization that makes people who they are. Someone else's frame of reference might not compute right and wrong the way you see it, and respecting that is the first step in correctly identifying what frame of reference you're working with.

A good support system essentially becomes a safe harbor where we find refuge. The feeling of advocacy and support helps keep us grounded in determining where we fit in the scheme of society. As toddlers, trusting that someone will pick us up when we fall helps instill in us trust and hope in the world around us and belief in ourselves. Later, someone being there for us as we experience life challenges reinforces that trust and hope.

Your frame of reference can either become affirmative, or it can have negative consequences, depending in great measure on the support or lack thereof from family and friends. When we don't have the security and influence of strong family bonds early in life, the groundwork is laid for making choices that lead to destructive measures. If we aren't loved as children, we may later seek love and acceptance in ways that lead us to addiction, depression, abuse, unsustainable relationships, or even criminal behavior. There is a deep yearning to fill that hollowness residing in the heart and soul from a lack of love, acceptance, and appreciation.

Make no mistake, you can take action to reverse the effect of negative support from your extended family, but first you have to own it. You have to say, "OK, so I didn't come from the best background. I didn't have the best support system. But today, right now, I am going to acknowledge it and move forward. It is my responsibility to end any dysfunctional cycle and make better choices for myself today."

Whether the support of your extended family comes across as positive or negative, it's vital to say, "I'm committed to surrounding myself with positive, genuine people. I'm committed to seeking out friends and family members who are positive in their outlook."

Here is the bottom line: You cannot let a lack of support in your past dictate your future. You have to have the strength to demand positive, meaningful support from the people in your world. If you can't, you have to have the strength to move past those people.

A strong support of family and friends helps us to thrive in all aspects of life, but I think it is important to state it in no uncertain terms. This support is a key component to your frame of reference. Keep your support positive and make sure the people in your support group are people who BELIEVE in you as much as you believe in yourself.

Self-Assessment: Extended Family Support

Who provides your immediate support outside of yourself? (e.g. family, friends, spouse) What is it that you get from these people?

Example 1: My best friend always provides positive support for me. He will always be completely honest and forthright with me.

Example 2: My mother is always there for me. She is my biggest advocate and cheerleader.

_____

_____

_____

_____

_____

Whom do you look to for advice? (e.g. family, friends, spouse, pastor,) Explain why.

Example 1: I look for advice from my mentor. He always introduces me to tremendous life experiences and shows me how to use them in a positive way.

Example 2: I look for advice from my minister because I know I need to maintain a strong spiritual foundation.

_____

_____

_____

_____

_____

Answer this. An ideal support system for me includes…(e.g. family, friends, and relatives)

Example 1: The ideal support system would include my parents because they helped shape who I am.

Example 2: The ideal support system would include my spouse because our shared experience can contribute to a more complete life.

_____

_____

_____

_____

_____

Describe what you need from your support system (examples could be encouragement, honesty, love, support, positive reinforcement), and indicate if you are getting it. If not, develop an action plan for either making adjustments to your support system or making sure you get and maintain what you need.

Example 1: I need complete honesty from my support group. I don't need my friends or family to say what they think I want to hear. I need them to go to the heart of the matter and know they are acting in my best interest.

_____

_____

_____

_____

_____

Values and Beliefs

The next concept in determining your frame of reference involves an honest assessment of your values and beliefs. Values are the building blocks of your internal compass. Values are those things that matter to you more than anything. Values are what you hold in high regard.

If you have to make an important personal or professional decision in your life, your values are what you call upon in doing so.

I list a few of my values as honesty, integrity, character, professionalism, and ethics.

Coupled with our behavior, our emotions and feelings, our life experiences, our image of self, and our environment, values and beliefs are yet another foundation piece in the BELIEVE model. They impact our frame of reference and nudge us closer to answering the question, who do you think you are?

You measuring tool for your place in the world, and that tool consist of the values you hold dear (e.g. acceptance, beauty, determination). Your fundamental beliefs fuel your decision-making and dictate your behavior. Therefore, the more in tune you are to your values, the more aware you become.

Your values are a culmination of everything that has happened to you in life. They include influences from your parents and family, religious affiliation, friends and peers, education, reading, and more. As I have stressed throughout this book, it is vital for you to take the time to recognize the environmental influences. Once you've done that, the next step is to consciously develop a clear, concise, and meaningful set of values and beliefs. Once defined, values will impact most of your life choices. They are the barometer driving your actions in the world.

From childhood through adolescence, values are instilled in us. People, events, and situations influence us and forge our beliefs. It can't be helped.

As an adult, you are now in a position to reassess your values and alter them, if need be, to fit the person you want to be.

I spent several years in corporate America with a company and served as a compliance manager. By the end of my tenure, I was acting as the company liaison with a local government agency. The company's upper management spent considerable time and energy making certain that we were all singing the same tune when the regulators started asking questions. The impression they wanted me to portray was that we were in complete compliance with the regulations in question. Too bad we weren't.

As the company liaison, I agonized over management's insistence that we fudge the truth. It was in complete opposition to my value system. The good news is that my value system won out. The even better news was that I resigned my position shortly thereafter and went on to start my own business, a business completely in tune with my personal values and beliefs.

As an adult, you demonstrate your values in action. They are reflected in your behavior, both personal and professional. Values are a deciding factor when it comes to your interpersonal interactions. Even your goals and life purpose are grounded in your values.

For example, if you set a goal to lose 20 pounds, the nagging feeling that you get when you bend the rules of the diet is an effect of your values being tested and compromised.

If you alter the facts of your resume to influence a job interview, rest assured that the guilt you feel stems from your values trying to set the record straight.

When considering your frame of reference, choose the values that are most important to you—the values you believe will define your character when no one else is around. You should then live them visibly—every day. Living your values is one of the most powerful tools there is when it comes to being the person you want to be. It is equally powerful when it comes to accomplishing your goals and dreams. If your dream is to lead, if you hope to have a positive influence on the lives of your peers, then living your values is the best way to start.

Your values are exemplified in your character. Your character is what people see. The decisions that you make and your nonverbal communication such as your posture and even the way you walk sends a message to people the depth of your character, and you want this outward appearance to truly reflect the person inside.

When you haven't identified or clearly defined your values, you end up day-dreaming your life away. Instead of basing your decisions on an internal compass, you make choices based on circumstances and social pressures. You end up trying to fulfill other people's expectations instead of your own. Before you know it, life has passed you by, and you haven't even started to live. Trying to be someone else and living without positive core values are downright exhausting. It leaves you lacking in self-worth and feeling empty.

Living a life in line with your core values, on the other hand, brings purpose, direction, happiness, and wholeness to a well-rounded frame of reference.

You would be surprised by how many people are stuck when asked to list their values. If you haven't *clearly* defined yours, you can end up making conflicting choices, and when your actions conflict with your values, the result is unhappiness and frustration.

I know that when I take the time to meditate upon my values, I'm more likely to have the courage and confidence to make choices based on those values. It begins, however, with the process of identifying your values, of actually putting a name to them, of writing them down to formalize the process. I know from experience that writing down your values makes you more committed to living them.

So what do you value most? Honesty?.. Integrity?.. Creativity?.. Loyalty?.. Respect? As you consider your values, ask yourself, "Is this the way I want to live my life? Are these values in line with my internal compass? Does this set of values and beliefs work best for me in my journey to live my best life? Finally, will these values move me to action?"

If all your answers are "yes," you are on your way to the greatness you were meant to have.

Self-Assessment: Values and Beliefs

As you look back over your life, describe what values and beliefs have kept you grounded and why.

Example 1: Responsibility. I was taught early on by my father that it is a man's job to care for his family in all situations.

Example 2: Self-love. I saw how much pride my mother had in herself despite coming from humble beginnings, and it inspired me as a woman.

_____

_____

_____

_____

_____

What is the one major thing that has influenced your values? (This could actually be a person; if so, describe what that relationship was like.)

Example 1: My grandparents. They came to this country from less than ideal backgrounds and built a life for themselves.

Example 2: My mom took my sister and me to a homeless shelter to help serve food to the poor, and I never took what I had for granted after that.

_____

_____

_____

_____

_____

A positive personal belief I have about life is…

Example 1: A man has to put honesty above all else.

Example 2: As a mother, I will make certain that my children understand the value of respecting their elders.

_____

_____

_____

_____

_____

Values and beliefs are important to me because...

Example 1: They are the compass that guides me even in the most trying of times.

_____

_____

_____

_____

_____

Have there been any negative influences or experiences in your life that affected your core values and beliefs? If so, describe them below, and develop an action plan on how you intend to change that view.

Example 1: We were poor. My father stole for food instead of looking for a job. I know now that I have to work hard for everything I get, and I will do everything I can to continue to grow as a person.

_____

_____

_____

_____

_____

E̲nvironment

The physical environment that you find yourself in every day has an impact on your life. With that in mind, let's recall our definition: your frame of reference is where you are in your life at any time based upon everything that has happened to you and all the environmental and cultural beliefs that have made you the person that you are. Environment is not only vital to your frame of reference: it is the last concept in our BELIEVE model. It is also the last concept we need to discuss in answering the question, who do you think you are?

Please understand that your "environment" is multifaceted. When we speak of environment, we are talking about your physical living space both past and present. It also includes the schools you attended; the parents or guardians who raised you, the children you played with, and the people who scared you, made you laugh, or caused you to think. Your environment consists of more than the physical things and people in your life. Environment is also emotional, psychological, and spiritual. It is literally what is going on inside your subconscious mind.

In our BELIEVE model, we put environment last because all the other components play so heavily upon it. Your behavior is hugely contingent upon your environment. Your emotions and feelings paint your environment a certain color. Your life experiences all come to bear on your environment. Your image of yourself dictates how you look at your environment. Your values and beliefs give you power in making decisions about your environment.

Let's look at two examples…

A young girl grows up in a household where hard work ethic is a common practice every day. She sees her parents practicing what they preach in their own jobs. Today, that very prominent work ethic permeates this young woman's professional environment and her commitment to success.

A young boy grows up in the aftermath of hurricane Katrina and observes his parents subsidizing from government outreach programs. He grows up struggling with the concept of community and self-determination and finds it hard to adjust when he moves to another city, where he's forced to make it by himself.

The girl in our first example grows up in a home that places little emphasis on religion or spirituality. As a young adult, she finds it hard knowing where to put her faith when a good friend dies at an early age.

On the other hand, the Bible was the only book in the home where the boy in our second example grew up. Faced with the same tragedy as the girl, his current environment, while difficult in many respects, provides him with a spiritual base that helps him cope with his lose.

In other words, everyone has pros and cons gained from past and present environments. The key is the positive attitude that you bring to each situation going.

To demonstrate how the environment is more than the physical, consider your workplace. Your environment is not only *where* you work and the people you work with, but it is the trust (or lack thereof) that your boss shows in you and the fun (of lack thereof) you have with your peers.

You could move from the worst company in the world to one of the best, and your choice can lead to an emotional reaction of either elation to watchfulness—all because of the environment you left behind.

One major factor in your environment is your support system. From your siblings at home to your roommate in college, the relationships that you build affect your environment. You could live in a ramshackle house with five college roommates and feel like the luckiest person on the planet. A woman I recently counseled grew up in an abusive home—as both victim and witness. Her only refuge was a crawl space in the basement of her family house, where she spent many hours huddled in fear. As a young woman, she and her husband were looking for a new house in a new city, when they came upon a place that looked perfect in all respects. While touring the house, they went into the basement, and the crawl space was a dead ringer for the one in which she had hidden herself so often in her youth. The memory, long suppressed, was so strong that the "perfect" home was now unacceptable, and the couple had to cross it off their list.

A hostile voice from the past can be resurrected by a similar voice in the present, just as a comforting one can. The same can be said for a scent, a taste, or even a touch.

Our environments can be complicated places with unique history, but we are not servants too our environment. If you are unwilling to leave a lousy job, you can determine to make it the best it can possibly be. If the economic market makes it impossible to sell your current home, you can make changes within it that make it more homelike.

Because of the enormous impact that environment has, it behooves us to seriously consider making positive adjustments when it is in our power to do so. This is often easier said than done, in particular with regard to your physical environment, but you always have the power of choice. You always have the personal ability to stay positive.

One trick I often employ is to think of my current home environment as a place where solace and peace are close at hand. When I want to take time out away from the pressures of society or the rumblings of the outside world, I simply go to a dedicated place and meditate. It could be the back porch or an old couch in the basement. I create an environment within an environment. It is a conscious choice that empowers me to control my environment and look out for my own best interest.

Look around your home and consider a place that you can go and shut the world out. Take fifteen or twenty minutes to unwind, relax, and regroup. Do the same at work when possible.

If there are people, by necessity, always in your environment, make sure their influences are genuinely enhancing your frame of reference.

If you have been consumed by an environmental history that you no longer care for, I suggest you to take some time now and start giving that experience new meaning for yourself. Use your personal power to choose differently. Start with positive self-talk to help rid yourself of those negative programs in your mind. Tell yourself that any negative environmental history will no longer define your current environment. Direct your energy to positive experiences and don't deviate. Why? Your frame of life depends on it, and it is your frame of reference that gives you the power to act, and to be your own best friend.

Self-Assessment: Environmental Factors

How does the environment I live in affect my self-image?

Example 1: I am in an abusive relationship, which has left me with a fragile, self-deprecating self-image.

Example 2: My home was filled with entrepreneurial energy that gave me the confidence to start my own business.

_____

_____

_____

_____

_____

Develop an action plan of improving your environment or making choices that will benefit you going forward. It is all about the greatness you deserve.

Example 1: I will no longer allow a certain member of my family to make disparaging remarks about myself, my siblings, or my children.

Example 2: I will make it clear to my boss at work that his lack of respect for my contributions to our team will no longer go unchallenged.

_____

_____

_____

_____

_____

Self-Discipline

You may be asking, Why a chapter on self-discipline when the subject has been covered many times and from a number of different perspectives? The answer is simple: In your search to recognize your frame of reference, self-discipline is an absolutely essential tool. In fact, self-discipline is key in answering the question, who do you think you are? Self-discipline is also a key action point in working with the BELIEVE model.

We've all had conversations with ourselves about self-discipline. In most cases the conversation revolves around having too little. Sometimes the matter at hand is something as simple as quitting a bad habit. It could also be the attainment of a strongly desired life goal, the achievement of a new objective, or a change to your current way of thinking. It all takes self-discipline.

E*very one* of us is capable of self-discipline. It is not a matter of some people having it and some not. We all have the mental capacity, but it is a matter of choice.

The bottom line is that *you* control your behavior. A common approach to tackling self-discipline is to consider even our smallest actions as steps in the direction of life-changing behavior. Consider this very effective, yet relatively simple, exercise. Pick something you would like to change about yourself. It could be something as straightforward as getting up a half hour earlier every day, cutting your nightly television by a half hour, doing some type of exercise every day. Then commit to doing that something every day for a week.

Make a rule that for every day you miss, you'll add two days to the end of that week. This exercise is behavior-based, but your success or failure can be tied directly to your frame of reference.

As part of the exercise, take a moment and consider all you could accomplish if you could just get yourself into action and follow your best intentions, no matter what the circumstances. Why is this often so difficult? The silent word is "motivation." Other people can inspire and influence you to set goals and take action, but they cannot motivate you. People often say that a great leader or an effective speaker can motivate a person to do more or work harder or be more committed. This is a fallacy. Great leaders and effective speakers can *inspire* you. They can influence you. But the motivation to act comes from within. You have to *own* your motivation.

When you truly know the answer to the question—who do you think you are?—then you will understand what motivates you and what does not. The better you know yourself, the more you will recognize your true motivations.

As a life coach and public speaker, I can only hope to inspire people to act. I can hope to influence their thinking in a positive way. But I cannot instill motivation. That is self-directed. The good news is that you have all the tools you'll ever need to motivate yourself. When motivation is driven by positive internal factors, it carries more weight and more power.

That being said, it is essential to recognize that very few things in life come to us obstacle-free. As a life coach, I always encourage my clients to consider their goals in light of what I call the "obstacles to success." Anticipating distractions and stumbling blocks to self-discipline is one of the most important tools I can share.

When you've anticipated an obstacle to success, you're far less likely to fall victim to it when it presents itself. For example, exercise. Let's assume your goal is some form of daily exercise, and your plan is to join a neighborhood gym. OK, what things might get in the way of your daily exercise plan or hinder your progress? Ask yourself this question ahead of time and have an action plan in place to overcome the obstacles. What happens if I've partied too hard the night before and can't drag myself to the gym in the morning? Solution: pick an hour in the early evening after work and commit to going without fail. What happens if my car dies, and I can't get to the gym? Solution: plan on taking a jog around the neighborhood or a half-hour walk in the park. What happens if I have to work overtime at my job? Solution: commit to an abbreviated workout after you get off, even if it means sacrificing an hour of television time.

You can think of a dozen examples, but the point is to develop an action plan to overcome any obstacles and employ the action plan when self-discipline starts slipping. Make sure to write down both your potential obstacles and your plan to overcome them. And finally, hold yourself accountable.

A pinnacle moment in self-discipline is when you realize that you and you alone, are in control of your thoughts and behaviors. When you realize that, the follow-through on your goals, wants, and desires will happen almost unconsciously. You'll be able to employ self-discipline no matter what your emotional state may be. The circumstances might change, but the tools remain the same.

Then you can look at your behavior, your emotions and feelings, your life experiences, your environment, your image of self, your values and beliefs, and your extended family and support system—all the elements of our BELIEVE model—and make conscious choices as to their impact on your frame of reference. Then you will be a person in control of your life and your destiny.

Consider self-discipline as a means of empowerment, one that you can always strive for on the road to personal development. Since we all are traveling the road to success, it's important to remember just how big self-discipline plays a role in getting you where you are today. Some may see progress now, and some may have a ways go to. The important thing is to keep moving toward the greatness you deserve.

Now that we have delved into the BELIEVE model, I compel you to consider what drives your behavior. Each of the concepts we explored in the previous chapters contributes to your makeup as a person and defines who you are today.

Your frame of reference is your conscious mind, and your thoughts are what dictate your emotions, feelings, and, ultimately, how you behave. When questions arise as to why you feel a certain way or are doing certain things, you have the tools now to retrace your steps as far back as you need to, whether the journey takes you back an hour or all the way back to your childhood. I am sure you will find that it was one of the BELIEVE concepts that brought you to this place in time, right here, right now.

Now at last you have your answer. Who do you think you are?

Summary

The BELIEVE model is not theoretical. Many of my clients have used it successfully in their search for their frames of reference. I used it to figure out my own frame of reference.

My search began twenty-five years ago when, as a teenager, I found myself so depressed that I contemplated ending my life at one point. I felt unloved and didn't love myself. I had very few friends. I really did not trust anyone. When I looked in the mirror, I did not like the person I saw. My self-image was based on what others thought of me, and my self-esteem was essentially nonexistent.

I had one thing going for me. I loved to write. It was the journals I kept over the years that inspired my BELIEVE model. Writing proved to be the one place where I could safely and freely open my heart. My journal never judged me—it just told me who I was.

I discovered—in the writing and the rereading of hundreds and hundreds of pages—a person with as many bright moments as dark moments, with as many ups as downs. I discovered a person searching for an answer to the question, who am I?

Why do I feel this way? How do I get out?

Mediation and prayer helped. Observation and study helped. However, the search for my frame of reference still took fifteen years. After all that time, I realized I was a person in control of my thoughts, feelings, and emotions. I could determine my values and live them fully. I could use my life experiences to make me a better man. I began to understand that all the baggage from my past need not impact my life going forward. I realized I was a man in charge of his own behavior, and nothing could be more empowering.

Today, my support system is better than it has ever been because I have chosen it for myself. I decide on a daily basis that no single negative situation gets all of my positive energy, and that helps me to live a much healthier life. No one other than God has more power than I do in my life. My self-image is off the charts, and my self-esteem is unwavering

I can look at myself in the mirror and see a man of integrity with sound values and beliefs. I love who I am, and I love what God has done in my life. I am now an educator, a life coach, a mentor, and a family man. I live each day on a mission to give back what life has given me.

It is my hope that understanding the concepts presented in this book will help someone find and maintain their greatness. The BELIEVE model is a daily exercise, but one that delights and inspires with practice. The BELIEVE model is about self-determination, and the more you practice it, the less likely any person or any circumstance will create negative influence over your life.

When you know that both the positives and negatives in your life are reflected in your frame of reference, you will use every experience and emotion to carve out a beautiful value system and an image of self that will positively impact your behavior in the most intense way imaginable.

You will come out of this wonderful journey a stronger and wiser person and one with an unwavering determination to live a better life. That is priceless.

You have greatness within you that is just waiting to be unleashed. That greatness can and will shine in your walk and even casual conversation. Make it a way of life. Know always that you are headed in the direction of personal and professional fulfillment, regardless of your circumstances.